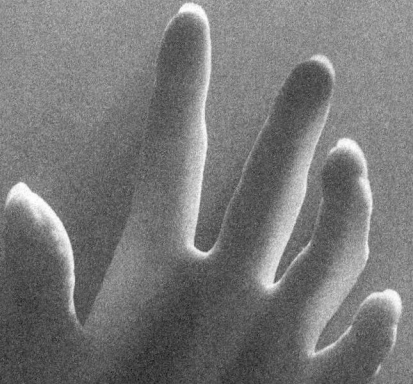

SACRIFICIAL STEEL
CATE MCGOWAN

Independently published by *Driftwood Press*
in the United States of America.

Managing Poetry Editor & Interviewer: Sara Moore Wagner
Cover Image: Justin Limke
Cover Design: Sally Franckowiak
Interior Design: James McNulty
Copyeditor: James McNulty
Fonts: Knockout, Merriweather, & Alternate Gothic Extra
Condensed

Copyright © 2025 by Cate McGowan
All Rights Reserved.

No part of this publication
may be reproduced, stored in a retrieval
program, or transmitted, in any form or by
any means (electronic, mechanical,
photographic, recording, etc.), without
the publisher's written permission.

First published June 17, 2025
ISBN-13: 978-1-949065-35-0

Please visit our website at www.driftwoodpress.com
or email us at editor@driftwoodpress.net.

PRAISE FOR
SACRIFICIAL STEEL

"A wonderful addition to contemporary poetry, Cate McGowan's *Sacrificial Steel* cuts lyric vision with punk swagger and mordant humor to examine womanhood, history, family, ecological disaster, and Southern identity. I am gobsmacked by the precision and restraint that characterize these impeccable poems—every syllable, every character, every space. Like her contemporaries, feminist poets Cynthia Cruz and Aracelis Girmay, McGowan possesses a fine intelligence that is matched only by her conscience. These poems affirm that it is now, as it has been, the poet's work to 'clock the universe's massacres, dark / soffits, underhanded sky.'"

—Carolyn Hembree,
author of *For Today*

"*Sacrificial Steel* is as much a song of grief as it is ekphrasis of the art of survival. Steered by a guiding belief in the poet's role as musician and artist, Cate McGowan's debut collection dexterously navigates a range of human experience—from the specter of death in one girl's family to the ravages of our collective human impact on the natural world. On every page, McGowan witnesses the mixed bag of who we are—loving and leaving, violent and tender: 'We're corpuscles and kidneys, sweat and shit and spit,/ admixtures, fragile parts in fancy wrappings'—and calls us to resist the 'magnetism of demise.' 'Nothing's discouraged me,' the poet says. 'I shouldn't exist, yet I'm here.' Read this one slowly. Savor its music."

—Cynthia Marie Hoffman,
author of *Exploding Head*

"*Sacrificial Steel* is a stunning debut collection, bright as a lighthouse flashing into the dark. These poems hide from nothing, illuminating truths about both the vicious and beautiful possibilities of our world. They embody the sublime and are breathtaking in their precise candor."

— Erica Wright,
author of *All the Bayou Stories End with Drowned*

CONTENTS

I.

FOLD THE SHADOWS	3
CUTS	5
A SLIP JIG AND REEL IN CUT-TIME	7
CATECHISM *OR* PARTING PANTOUM	8
FALLING IS THE DEADEST THING	10
MOTHER COURAGE	11
THE SYMPATHY OF CLOCKS	12
RSVP IS THE COLLECTIVE NOUN FOR SNOWY EGRETS	15
DEPENDING ON THE HORIZON	17
DANCE THIS MESS AROUND	18
UNRHYMED SONNET CONSTRUCTED WITH AMERICAN SENTENCES	19
FOR MY MOTHER, WHO IS DEAD, BUT SPENT TOO LONG DYING	20

II.

LEAVES AIM TOWARD THUNDER	25
LOPSIDED	26
EVERY BODY HAS GHOSTS	27
SPOOKY LITTLE THINGS	29
CHYRONS RUN THROUGH MY HEAD 1	30
SING AWAY, MY SISTER	32
PSYCHO	35
RECKONING	36
THINGS I NEVER SAID	37
LOVE IS A GRAVEYARD FOR THE LONELY *OR* PASTORAL	38
EMBRACE LIGHT, ADMIRE IT, LOVE IT	39

III.

THANKSGIVING, SUNSET	45
RETURN	46
IF ONLY I COULD CHOOSE MY OWN COUNTRY,	47

THE LIVES I SAVE ARE NEVER MY OWN	49
A NEWSPAPER HEADLINE ANNOUNCES THAT THE BIG BANG CREATED A MIRROR UNIVERSE WHERE TIME GOES BACKWARD	51
INAUGURAL POEM, JANUARY 20, 2001	52
PROOF THROUGH THE NIGHT	56
THE WORLD WILL BLOW	57
GHAZAL FOR A DISPIRITED PLACE	58
LESSON PLAN	59
CHYRONS RUN THROUGH MY HEAD 2	61

IV.

DARK KNOTS	65
PREDICAMENT	66
IN MARGHERITA'S KINGDOM, A VILLANELLE	67
SHORTEST COMPLETE SENTENCE IN THE ENGLISH LANGUAGE	68
QUIET MOMENTS DESERVE HEROES	69
HUNTERS & COLLECTORS	72
CONSEQUENCES IN WATER	74
INEFFABLE	75
RESURFACE	76
THE LOON WAILS THIS MORNING	77
INTERVIEW: QUIET OBSERVATION, DECAY, AND THE VIOLENCE SIMMERING UNDER THE SURFACE OF THE ORDINARY	79

*I am circling around God, around the ancient tower,
and I have been circling for a thousand years,
and I still don't know if I am a falcon, or a storm,
or a great song.*

— Rainer Maria Rilke

*See the handsome mourners crying
They hawked a beating heart for a sturdy spine.*

— Fontaines D.C., "Jackie Down the Line"

*'Cause when love is gone
There's always justice
And when justice is gone
There's always force
And when force is gone
There's always Mom, hi Mom*

— Laurie Anderson, "O Superman"

FOLD THE SHADOWS

Yes, at first, I tried brevity,
used contractions, looked
for substitutions of formal

constructions. *Won't* replaced
maybe after the night a stranger
split me, when I curled small

in my Honda. Words like *shouldn't*
squatted, & I refused to abandon
them. Years passed. On a mission,

I truncated my expressions—
I added *can't* & *didn't* to *won't*.
My shortcomings added up;

they elongated my mother's
drawling disapproval. No one
listened. A witchy chorus

of skeptics hovered on broomsticks.
Why should someone believe
me, anyway? Midnight tonight

in a desolate meadow. In the distance,
orange groves burn. I study moths
with fellow lepidopterists. A kid

asks, *What gives us value? Is it breath?
Or goodwill?* He watches me tend
to a grey insect struggling

in the confines of its thin net,
scrapping through the early
morning flashlight penumbras,

tugged toward death. Oh, the magnetism
of demise—it's irresistible tonight.
Those long-leaf pines slash their own

shadows. Yet still, I battle elisions
that lurk in gravitas, & I employ
diction no one gets. Words

like *victim* transcend this page turn's
tectonics. I still possess power,
but I'm diminished by bulges & bad

knees. I can summon a summer
night from memory, weave spells
that hearken back to the evil taste

of a .45 on my tongue. I conjure
ruin out of *nothing* when *nothing* pleats
spectral places, those ensorcelled

hours when slavering devils howl
toward morning. With my old-fangled
magic, *I'm* self-destructs to *I am*

not. Chilling verbs act & wink
& flirt & force & command.
They slide over from the passenger

seat, & the phantom of my rapist
uncrimps. There's no trick to forgetting
terror, to losing that midnight,

that time I lay prone on my vinyl
backseat, inhaling my attacker's
four-day-old scent. The shortest

complete sentence in the English
language never chases away
the horror or my mother's shame.

No.

CUTS

Today, I fashion a scarf from your seven braids,
weave a coverlet of sorrows. The warp: tresses

you once molted on my pillow. The weft:
black-wire strands, hair I'd tug as you

entered my tent. Not so long ago (or was it
long ago?), ruthless Philistines tricked me

into believing their twined tales. So, I barbered
you, and your slick plaits slithered to the floor,

slapping the warm tiles. It was done.
Your strength scattered to the desert's corners.

Dusk disappeared, too, like a night storm,
azure curling, buffeting the horizon.

My servants held you down. And then I carved
out your eyes. Oh, how I've grown to regret

my sécateur cuts—you no longer plant seeds
inside my kingdom. And fallow fields are useless,

aren't they? Now, we lounge in our charnel-
like pavilion, and you shift, dry joints crackling

on the divan, and you complain about the bitter
wine, pinkie hooked as you sip last year's harvest.

I comb your ringlets into my loom, gossip about
the battles out there, chariot races, army marches

you've missed. But you're distracted. Your frail
frame moves toward the open window, and the lace

curtains cloud around you. Your fingers flit
and swat at phantoms, and you trace the crewel

on your embroidered tunic, grip the railing.
How a warrior wastes into an idea. Muscles unmarbled.

Bones brittle. Breakable. You face the sky, eye sockets
escutcheoned, cirrus speeding away, and you fly.

A SLIP JIG AND REEL IN CUT-TIME

Daddy dogs with the coal boys,
clocks the loose-planked floor
with his boot. Resin dust rises,
gambols to "Jayman's Stomp."
A bodhrán beats time for
the generations, while ghosts
of fiddle and pennywhistle
do-si-do in the lamplight.

History's crackled record
is mine now with its patchy verses.
The needle taps on the player,
gavottes a Georgia reel, skips
through. I inherit the two-step
tune on the tin speakers,
and the Bremer polka bops
out the open window.

Tonight, Daddy's frets slide
to me across the shadows,
and I clog in 9/8 time,
hum from the dark side of the door.

CATECHISM *OR* PARTING PANTOUM

I lose my faith at my father's funeral.
      Pallbearers pace, and the dolly wheels whine.
Spades. Clumps from a yawning hole. On my father,
      a spray, lilies, Mom's anthurium arrangement.

      Pallbearers pace. And the dolly wheels whine—
the creaky rig cradles Dad's slow coffin.
      A spray of lilies, Mom's anthurium arrangement
jostles. Sad flowers girdle and adorn

the creaky rig. Cradle Dad, slow coffin.
      Mom's rosary slips through her fingers,
jostles sad flowers. Girdled and adorned,
      she mouths the Sorrowful Mysteries, dolor.

      Mom's rosary slips. Through her fingers,
whispered grief. Handkerchief. *Holy is His Name,*
      she mouths, sorrowful, mysteries' dolor,
as she yanks me toward the gaping grave,

whispers, grief, handkerchief holy. Is his name
      my father's, who was mangled, closed-casketed?
As she yanks me toward the gaping grave,
      what's an awkward kid of nine to do?

      My father who *was*. Mangled, (closed-casketed),
supine inside a varnished pine box, its knots pouting.
      What's an awkward kid of nine to do?
I'm stuck here. The descending vessel's black patterns swirl

supine inside a varnished pine box. It's not pouting.
      My father's gone; he's nothing. In there,
I'm stuck. Here, descending, the vessel's black. Patterns swirl.
      A cloud shadows, and Monsignor Moore prays

       my father's gone—*He's nothing in there.*
Rites, benisons, and the litanies. *All flesh is grass.*
         A cloud. Shadows. And Monsignor Moore prays
over the void. We lean through Our Fathers,

rites. Benisons and the litanies' flesh is grass's
       past. Moments. Above, roots, above. The green
over the void we lean through. Our father's
       last ceremony, and I gawk at springtimes

       passed. Moments, above roots, above the green
blown dogwood. Blossoms rasp. In a stiff-gust
       last ceremony, I gawk. At springtime's
empty pageants, nature's the only thing that matters.

Blown dogwood blossoms rasp in a stiff gust.
       The gravedigger spits, then grabs a shovel.
Empty pageants—nature's the only thing that matters,
       not their hollow salvations and resurrections.

       The gravedigger spits then, grabs a shovel,
spades clumps from a yawning hole onto my father
       not there. Hollow salvations and resurrections—
I lose faith at Daddy's burial.

FALLING IS THE DEADEST THING
A CENTO

All day long, we are in love with water.
I don't want to say anything. What
of love's austere and lonely offices
late in a spring that has no age?
I think this year I will wait for the white lilacs,
for the grass to catch fire.

I glimpse you from the window, striding toward the river
that carries me through the clear day.
I hear someone, hear the splash, groan,
where, against a background of chirping birds,
no one is blessed with deafness here.
Heavier things are up and falling
when the spade sinks into gravelly ground:
water, stone, wind,
homesickness that guides the plovers.

Once, I nudged a canoe through that water—
what did I know, what did I know?
The smile on your mouth was the deadest thing.
I didn't fall in love. I fell through it:
a concordance of person, number, voice.
Later, *on the day you fell through a cloud,*
it felt right to be up this close in tight wind.

No, says water in that limpid voice,
nicking and slicing neatly, heaving sods.
It seems, for a moment, the river ceases flowing
before I get too sad.

MOTHER COURAGE

> *Wherever life has not died out / it staggers to its feet again.*
> —Bertolt Brecht, *Mother Courage and Her Children*

War-earned silence moves through
our house. Hope vanishes into closets;
   the quiet drifts graceful as a canoe,
seaworthy, rotatable, never overturned.
Soldiers' apparitions haunt our stairs—

travel down, not up. And my husband
wears soft shoes on these hard floors.
   An officer with waxed whiskers.
On Sundays, I brush his blazer, polish
the brass buttons. I scrub the pots

he brought me from Belgium, the copper
sheen of adventure dulled by this gray
   wife in a two-lane town. On garbage
Wednesdays back in the city, I woke to
the din of machine music, ratamacues.

Burring trucks, ashcan tunes, workers' shouts.
Flamadiddles. Outside now, so far removed,
   along the cliff, a gale rises. But God
isn't here. I comb out my knots at the vanity,
but no braid works. No iron removes these

wrinkles. Nothing unpacks hope in the hall.
The wick spits, and the light dies as we push
   through evenings without power,
the gusts embouchuring taps, the branches
knocking, rat-a-tat-tatting the clerestory panes.

THE SYMPATHY OF CLOCKS

1. The Ship Navigator's Wife Tries Patience

The wet cave's a brackish tomb.
Slick with meaning, forgiveness

rustles in the ginnel's background.
I wonder about that incarnadine

atmosphere swirling cowlick
clouds, some sailor's delight.

Brothers' blood oaths. Fluorescence
of flowers and their bright

moon sweetness. The stars
quiver, tapping Morse patterns,

the patterns of wives' longing,
of ships gone, of soft evenings

lost, of no more pink skies at night.

2.   Dear Iona

My bonnie lass, how's tricks? From this Arctic
            journey, battle-on-the-seas sail, I send
you the jewels I have—sapphire Northern Lights
and red flak fire. Such colors! It's hard here
            near the pole where my compass rolls. I cram
cannons, count rounds. Great ordnances roar, spit,

            whine. They whistle tunes, clap clouds.
This war's at sixes and sevens, narrow squeaks.
            Orders come down each night: *Acquire targets.*
            Aim. Discharge! So, we launch missiles, salvos.
Threaded volleys timpani-thump, fling high.
            Disappeared shots crater boreal bowls,
pock the beaches, bust frigates, minesweepers.

            The tracers flick zenith bridges,
scoring Luftwaffe planes, the Messerschmitts
            pitching, diving like injured gulls. Their wrecks rain
green-glow debris, the seas swallowing fire.
I've forgotten why we are here fighting.
            Our bombs hit somewhere, kill somebody's someone.

Come the dawn's muster, we're dead-spent. Deaf, blind.
            White smoke whorls toward dark noon. Officers
bicker in their mess while deck crows scoot,
mad swells pitching, swashing the shouts, swabbed hulls.
            Signs and wonders come about—I perch
on the bridge, marvel at crowned auroras,
at the gibbous moon's half-veiled countenance.

            We pass navy fjords, iced peaks trinkling
like bobeched crystals in broken twilight.
When off-duty, through all-day barrages,
            I bury inside my bunk. Or I walk
the boat and search for smiles. No kind person
exists here. No one mentions wives or home.

Tonight, I watched whale pods surface, slick, black—
        their backs sprayed spume in lace-patterned fountains.
But pom-pommer half-wits aimed two-pounders,
shot the depths for U-boats. I yelled, *STOP!* They didn't.
        No fights are fair at the front.
        No fight's fair.

RSVP IS THE COLLECTIVE NOUN FOR SNOWY EGRETS

It's not easy to ignore a broken-necked bird
as I steer your wheelchair by the lake's edge.

Above us, a snowy egret's carcass contracts
and decays; it drapes in the crook of a cypress

bough. A valence of Spanish moss sifts
in gusts, a sort of chorus that caresses the bird's

deflated body, a kind of aeronautical feat.
Other than this passive flight, the corpse's

plumage is folderol. What about the rest
of the RSVP in the grove? They disregard

that limp form perched among them.
The congregation nests high, warming

their blanched wings in comfort. They preen,
keep on living as a corpse decomposes close by.

How can they trill so indolently, beaks
chewing at their quills of down? Folding

necks telescoping to groom glamorously
plump backs, long red streamer legs.

Oh, Mom, you're so quiet here, absorbing
the luster light, your head tilted back.

Your bones are eggshells; your lungs won't
abduct air. In six months, you'll be gone.

I'm cold, you complain. A ski boat passes,
and you flash a wave. *Hello!* Your eyes

are still bright, the blue color of deep water
on maps. Together, we trace the vessel's

ripples. The dock sighs, and we eavesdrop
on the whirring birds high in the trees.

DEPENDING ON THE HORIZON

Yes, the boys and I fashioned retrofitted, hand-me-down bikes—spray-painted speed machines tooled in overgrown backyards and empty garages; we made them tough like each of us, able to withstand Georgia red clay, easement trails, steep hills, improvised ramps. Those after-school afternoons, we pedaled muddy paths like the real Devil chased us. We scooted the creek-bank inclines, revving with hard steam and top-speeding our jumps; we'd slide to full stops on slick rocks, our damp windbreakers crayon bright against cloud backdrops. When we trimmed the humid atmosphere, hawk-like swiftness was our only concern. We stuck some landings but, most times, missed our marks to skid out, sporting rewards—dark-bruised knees or raspberried elbows. The boys and I panted through those faded afternoons and played on the clock as the cavernous woods swallowed us. We dreaded what was next—inevitable summons from home, supper songs wailing for us to return. Each mom's call had a particular lilt. A discrete rhythm canted and chanted. Come home to SUUU-pper! The tunes trilled over neighborhood rooftops from blocks away and stung our ears. Operatic choruses, sopranos and altos. The keens stalled us for a few seconds, and then we turned toward the melodies to acknowledge our doom. The dusky trees turned to blue shadows.

On those nights, the world nudged away our fun, and those family calls herded all the boys back home. Kyle and Chip and John and Ricky and Michael and Petey and Rusty. Each ten-year-old saddled up, peeled off, and left. When finally I was alone, I'd wait for my mother's reveilles. The cries seldom came. Instead, fall crickets conversed on the trail. I'd lean over my still wheels, kickstand-foot, ankles deep in orange mud, pine-straw pigtails warm nests against my back. I'd eye my target, mount my pedals, and lollygag back through the sky-dark forest. So much depended on the horizon and the stars piercing a purple vista. But the back-lit heavens were unreachable. Even then. Still, every night, I tried; I'd make a last go on a formidable rise, loft through the air, my scarlet jacket puffing a sail, and with no boys to mess with me, I soared like a hellkite, wheeling dangerous curves, tasting speed, the closest to joy I ever got. Or was the pleasure something else? With the glints of twilight, its freedom flashes. Behind were no siren songs to pull me back where I didn't want to go. No.

DANCE THIS MESS AROUND

At 14, I ripped fishnets, slammed, slash-danced, and crashed RuPaul
dance parties, Discotheque Au Go Gos; I hitched home at 5
to catch the school bus at dawn. In the back row, I preened, dolled
up the SPEDs, teased my bangs closer-to-God so I could arrive
at my locker hot, to wave like some royal slut on the lam.
I was that mean skank in AP Chem, that rad goth who pierced
her nipples, ice-numbed her darling buds, who bled when she jammed
push-pins through. What a pop. *Blitzkrieg bop!* These days, I'm not fierce.
Bangs before Botox is bullshit. *Gabba gabba hey's* not bona fide.
The kids I teach are hella bimbos bounding to E-cars,
their buff sig-Os parked in kiss lanes. Surfboard lives. Swag outside.
Prissy-priss Taylor Swifts—*I can't go for that. No can do!*
Yeah, I'm no wannabe. I was hot like you, fearless, fly,
all hopped up, ready to go. But time's a bitch. Time's sly.

UNRHYMED SONNET CONSTRUCTED WITH AMERICAN SENTENCES

After you turned ten, you tossed then lost pink clackers on low power lines.
That spring, rain-swelled creeks rose, an angry orange raging across your yard.
The woods brimmed like a sink basin, and your red playhouse slid off its blocks.
You pedaled home in another May cloudburst, scudded the muddy slopes.
Steering down the steep driveway, your soaked Schwinn's brakes failed, and you hit the wall.
Gears gone, wheels crimped, jaw cracked, chin gashed, you staggered, dragged a blood trail inside.
That ER visit drained the family savings. And your mom blamed you,
As usual, not the black clouds: *Girl, you've stirred trouble for the last time.*

Still not blessed, you plan to meet your divorce lawyer at the library.
You slow current the stacks where homeless men hide from summer—it's fucking hot.
Moisture from June humidity slinks in, loosens the glue on books' spines.
You think about making plans, but carrying an umbrella's pointless.
In Periodicals, you sweat tabloids about royal weddings.
Before your attorney arrives, you bail, blame yourself, the storms you've got.

FOR MY MOTHER, WHO IS DEAD, BUT SPENT TOO LONG DYING

I once believed mustachioed women
a commonplace & was sure I could grow
a beard if I wanted. I slipped out
of my seersucker dress when I played

with the boys through the moon landing
& our firefly chase, running from room
to room to hide from your switch.
I let the swing go & learned to welcome

the ground's arrival. I put my feet
on the ceiling in school: I was upside
down, & when I fell, I learned how
to fall with a pillow over my head,

cruel as a concrete sidewalk in dreams.
Did you know salt is a mineral? Neither
animal nor vegetable? Did you know
that salt is my favorite seasoning?

It *is* a season, like sweat. I learned
from you that intuition's more valued
than observation. I'm in your Georgia
garden, & in front of me is an overgrown

path. The broad beans are drying up
& brown. The sunset's keeping up
its act. I learned that dogs smell cancer
before we do. I learned that if you want

to be a victim, tell the truth. If you don't
want to be free, tell the truth. I learned
from you nothing is as sacred as the blood
in our veins, & blood thrusts through

our veins as a lie. You can't capture air
now; you won't live long. On this path
in the garden, trees breathe to explain
everything better than you can. Ahead,

a patch blooms with bees. Behind us,
the beds sag in fallowness. The lilies
perform to thunder that sings with feeling.
Without the bees, the lilies would fail.

Without rain, tender leaves wither.
Without me, you'd be alstroemeria
with undusted stamens as if part of all
of this; you'd be something if I were

not born. Someday, you'll hear me
before you see me—my voice, not
the sound of sleet. How could that be?
For years, you planted stalks no one

harvested. You watched them rise
tall. When the long stems collapsed,
& no one climbed, you buried
dry beans in your garden bed.

LEAVES AIM TOWARD THUNDER

*To love someone long-term is to attend a thousand funerals of
the people they used to be.*
— Heidi Priebe

Spring dithers, spurns its season, refuses
to muscle in. It suicides. The wrens abandon

three eggs on the stoop. Along the overgrown
path, a wondergarden sings with feeling, terrapins

sunbathe. Over there, red fern sprouts shoot first,
ask questions later and a scissor-tailed flycatcher

dives for a katydid. Those pines worry every minute
about this wind. In the warm kitchen, my fruit's

over-ripe, but I bite into the pear anyway, ponder
how your heart never conformed, how you never

noticed leaves aim toward thunder. A storm bangs
open; it racks the yard; the lilac molts pink petal

confetti as the parade of wet vehicles file past
on the road, the passengers' faces dull as worn-out coins.

You're merely an idea now, swaddled in white.
A brittle husk of memory. All the paintings disappear;

the water dries up for stars so bright they bleed.
I know lightning's unstable, but I'll call it what I will.

A charge of static, a frayed thread that stitches the air
and ground together—whatever that was between us,

a force with no name, a language we couldn't speak,
words not written. No words can capture that teeming,

fraught menace. Our words waited for invention that never
came.

LOPSIDED

For George Ohr, the Mad Potter of Mississippi

When this bowl cooled on the counter from the kiln,
your family laughed—*Crazy garbage!* So, you packed away
your creations in excelsior, forgot your hot aqua loves
in the barn. They called you strange and talentless, but you
threw their contempt on the wheel, spun your elaborate
containers. You once mused, *I have a notion that I am a mistake.*
But you knew a smooth surface cannot reveal beauty. Today,
beneath a museum's Plexiglass display, your bowl gleams,
its burnt umber finish shiny as Mississippi mud in springtime.
This lopsided vessel juts its belligerent lips, the sullen edges
Aquiline, quirky and useless as a tied-back
mustache. Inside the crock, your sad
thumbprints press floral lace
patterns, push away
the emptiness inside.

EVERY BODY HAS GHOSTS

Below a yellowed tree,
weeds fringe the driveway's
borders. Anoles pump.

They jut, and the bigger
lizards skitter along
the yard's edge. While

daylight's needles stitch
threads the spathodea,
seven De Kay's brown snakes

slue like scarves through
the new ivy. Though
it's already five o'clock,

I haven't heard from him
yet. Not this week.
Not this month. He's

gone with no word.
So far, silence. Green
quiet. Someone next door

opens a second-floor
window, and a toddler
shrieks, shatters the still air.

The child's cry skylarks
the mimosa, shrinks,
then dissipates through

the evening's haze. I shake
out our wet clothes.
In the breeze, the clothesline

snaps my red blouse
as it dances, my empty sleeves
waving in the wind to no one.

SPOOKY LITTLE THINGS

The day up & closes. A spiny
orb-weaver rappels the wall—
that spider from who-knows-where

mends gapes in her web,
tethers doomed
moths to lunch through

the night's sad hours, patient,
determined, pricking at strands
until her dawn retreat.

I'm not territorial like that.
No, I travel old corpse lanes,
sloped & tattered roads.

Where? Who knows? Who cares.
My headlights capture wraiths
at 3 AM. Cold spots. Shines.

Shucks are unwanted
travelers, phantoms who
wait to pass over, their faces

like ripped flags. I aim away
& my antennae catch faint
signals from far-flung places,

the crackles of DJs,
whose whispers stitch
somewhere towns

& highway nights
together. There, some
gods see stars.

CHYRONS RUN THROUGH MY HEAD 1

he
hollers   with the boys
saunters through   mile seven
and drags her porcelain dolls   nightmare fighters
who ignore her   evoke something   that isn't real

god needs to be pretty god needs to be pretty

remember
scandals rammed through ears
own the tales   through an attic hole   the moods
and veins   dark figures lingering along strewn gravel
and you must forget   must do that
somehow

god needs to be pretty just like you

dark figures linger   along
and you must forget   you must do that   somehow
more's the pity   pine for doses of dirt
so much for mirth   regret tastes strange
     lavished in hurt
reserve this feat
     for so much to brood

god needs to be pretty just like you

wounded like the wind   for a whole invention
whipped like a tail   let it spew
we watched you jump   intrude
     why dawn then   when
the world doesn't need news
     tarnished dark floors
          unmarked minds

god needs to be pretty   needs to be needed just like you

lost   in moments   lost and blind
tree limbs   noosed hair and eyes
    choose to tangle   see
        mingled surprise
thick ropes swing in a ferrous breeze
those scare tactics
    those heebie-jeebies

god needs to be nobody
    but you

SING AWAY, MY SISTER

> *This song of X-rays, coming from a chorus of millions of black holes, fills the entire sky.*
> —NASA's Jet Propulsion Laboratory,
> "Chorus of Black Holes Sings in X-Rays," 28 July 2016

Where does all the light go? Sister, is it sucked like matter into supermassive black holes,
pulled through eclipses & star fields to a doom

of darkness, a place where nothing escapes except X-ray music? The more
a black hole takes, the more it wants.

My sister, you ask, what do I know of robberies & cruelty? Oh, I know.
Planets, nebulae, far-flung quasars.

Crystal, silver, china, gold. Gone. Sister, you blew open the family safe.
You sang as you stole. Your soprano

sucked the energy from rooms, keened away with off-key phrases,
while I, the quiet alto on the front row,

mouthed harmonies, vibratoed my white dwarf warbles. I sit
on my back stoop & seethe about you,

admiring glamorous constellations where bodies orbit
whorling cores. A trick of the light.

The moon wanes, & a nightingale calls through a copse
at the pond's edge. At a space-age

distance, I clock the universe's massacres, dark
soffits, underhanded sky. Brutality's

acceptable, even beautiful, in the residue
of aftermaths, of orifices

dark, obsidian. Those chasms wrangle
yellow dwarves, red giants,

swallow fire after fire, snuff luminescence,
until all event-horizon evidence

disappears, the picked-off galaxies gobbled
whole through mine shafts.

The world sings aubades about density,
brags about building mass.

Apologies arrive too late now, vowels
on top of vowels, your

wavelength on a loop. Your serenades
burst energy as they

burgle, such raucous choruses only
observed/heard through

astronomers' special telescopes.
We lose so much to greed.

Sister, what a shame these naked
ears of ours, such weak

instruments, aren't alerted
to this universe's

rowdy record of carnage,
its score of astral

flashes, clicks & groans,
aural paisleys

airborne. Black-hole
bitch, stop

your whining. Sister,
stop your

high, low frequencies,
your X-ray

croons vespering,
speeding

away through
night.

Stop.

PSYCHO

[W]here I find myself surprised—and not so pleasantly surprised, more often than not, surprise instead into a heightened awareness of something troubling—
— Carl Phillips

The blonde actress plays herself as a redhead. Maybe
like in biopics I've watched too many times. I know
all the lines. Too unself-conscious for clichés, settings
unsettle stories. That memory remains something picked
at. The balled-up floss of reminiscence. What's left
of an Upstate winter so long ago. Yes, that memory.
Bathtub scum slick between my toes. Between my legs.
The plop of single drops from the faucet, acoustic effects
like film cues. Something troubling, something tragic
will materialize in the next frame. Mold flowers on the sink
and shelves. The papered ceiling's blossoms crane to catch
nakedness, and I slide inside the suds, inside the deep
basin. You swipe the fogged window with your sleeve.
The squeak's a harbinger.

RECKONING

Out here, it's not the dead grass where you sprayed
weed killer or the kidney-shaped pool burping
with algae. And it's not the girl who's half my age.
It's not my décollete that the makeup counter girl
says is crêped. It's not R.E.M. on the radio, our friend
Stipe's singing slurred. It's not even the shimmed
silence that wedged between us years ago. It's all
the moments we could have healed ourselves but didn't.
I wait for you to speak. The papers have not been signed.

All this isn't worth it, you say. You wave your hand
through the air, cigarette ash flying, the smoke a gauzy
legacy, and I glance over the neglected roofline, the house
we bought together, the life we had. I nod. *Yes, yes.
It's just stuff.* But I don't mean it. You grin. *The sky
has possibilities.* Your muted voice trails your last
drag as you exhale it across the neighbor's fence,
and we watch blinking planes traverse twilight.
The contrails bloat like sponges, dimple in the vista.

THINGS I NEVER SAID

> *Antiscian: noun—a person whose shadow at noon is cast in a direction contrary to that of an inhabitant of the other side of the equator living upon the same meridian*

I need the sound of your name, the rhythm
    of your vowels. I listen

for inhalations, for your antiscian
    breath. I'm trying to remember

what it's like to speak with someone,
    but I can't feel my tongue.

Even if I could, what would happen?
    We exist in different hemispheres.

I'd write you letters, but I'd have to wait
    for them to arrive across an equator.

Noon wakefulness. How dark's your sun?
    Your murmurs don't reach me.

But I could dig to China, and I wouldn't
    plow through your latitudes.

Below my window, figs in the over-full tree catch
    the gift of mid-day light. A single sparrow

calls alarm. I pivot away, peel an orange—tough skin
    tugged reveals so much juice inside.

I need this body.

LOVE IS A GRAVEYARD FOR THE LONELY *OR* PASTORAL

Arlington, North Military Road, 3000 block, 5:20 PM, Nov. 10, 2016. Responding to a call about an injured owl on the side of the road, an officer found a large mushroom.
—Local Section, "Animal Watch: An Unreal Animal Sighting,"
Washington Post, November 26, 2016

Early commuters and traffic exhaust. A police motorcycle
sputters to a stop on the median, parks. His radio blares,
the dispatcher's voice so hard to hear *...concerned citizen ... something ... owl.*
The cop fingers his Kevlar vest, draws out a can of tobacco, pokes
a wad into the pillow of his cheek. With his nightstick, he beats down
the tall grass under the streetlight, discovers a giant mushroom, not
the injured owl he expects. But birds are seldom what they seem. It's not
a dream, but near-dawn. In the verge's weeds, a blue-red strobe, the beacon
of enforcement. Three deer duck out of the traffic's headlight-beams, chomp
on the shoulder's fern shoots. Some scent wafts by. Cow manure from a farm
there across the highway. A truck horn honks, and a gust of startled sparrows,
a hooping flock, coils clockwise, eddies into a patch of elms. Moments
anchored to noise, chameleon hours—starlight closing shop to gold clouds.
The cop pops his kickstand, re-mounts his black motorbike, then booms away.

EMBRACE LIGHT, ADMIRE IT, LOVE IT

—*but above all, know light*, Mr. George Eastman once told me, and so, today, when no warmth remains, I can't stop thinking of that other February so long ago, its wind-scoured ice, the watery shadows, the weak sunshine, how you arrived at the orchid society's gathering with your plant to swap—it was a lady slipper, a *Cypripedium reginae*, who refused to flower (remember, you once asked me, *What good is a plant that never blooms?*), and after introductions at the get-together, you avoided small talk, declined hot tea served from the hostess's sterling samovar, ignored the shivering aspic, passed on the pastel *petit fours* the chef pyramided on china plates; instead, you wedged yourself splinter-straight into the farthest corner and studied the discarded cultivars on the sideboard (*leave a plant, take a plant*), studied the orchids in full flower (me) and the merely naked stems (your disappointing lady slipper), all the specimens waiting to be chosen, all unwanted, and then, the soirée's hostess, my grower, caught your eye, her purple hair swaying in a pharaoh-high pile, and she commanded you, *Take your turn, Mister Eastman,* and you paced, then halted in front of me as you admired my anther cap and velvety *labellum*, your sad eyes gray as an overcast winter morning, and you whispered, *Hello, my dear,* and my leaves stiffened at the timbre of your voice, and you rubbed a thumb down my spine, your ascot wiggling at your throat, blue serge suit lustrous under the chandelier, and you proclaimed, *I'll take this* Cattleya amethystoglossa, after which you snatched me and departed in haste, and we wandered home through a blizzard, me inside your coat, violet blossoms crushed close to your hard-beating heart, as you whistled a waltz by Strauss, regaling the Georgian estates and Tudor mansions, the dead perennial hedges as you kicked through the sidewalks' snowdrifts, the limousine following us at cortege speed; and that day was ages ago, but the light was like today's, like your eyes, and now, the power's out, and I'm awake early braving this ice storm, the downed power lines squiggling over the town's frozen walkways and sparking like camera flashes, and the illiquid cold vanquishes every plant in your conservatory, the sleet tap dancing a dirge across this behemoth manor's slate roof, above your kitchens where the overhead bulbs are dark, where no percolators pop and brew, where sweating condensation solidifies then crackles on the casements, and I gaze through that greenhouse glass at the clacking maples outside, their crystal-encrusted branches, upside-down icicle crowns that hold court outside the panes, and you won't throw tarpaulins over the mansard's hole, that fascia destroyed in last night's tempest, nor will you task the caretaker with the urgent repairs; instead, you perambulate, hum lullabies in this icebox orangery, and I wonder why you won't help my dying friends or me, your collection of beauties, the *Dendrobia, Oncidia, and Cymbidia, the Brassiae and Vandae,* the perfect, sickly-sweet smelling varieties, the scentless, the gamboge, citron, and chartreuse, all of us inhaling and exhaling what heat remains, but it's too frigid—thirty degrees Fahrenheit and dropping, twenty outside—and you rub my leaves, half-moaning, *It's no use . . .* while I crane to catch your breath's offerings, and I contemplate the world captured here, the impossible cloched daylight, the sepia tones that give me no hope, and I wonder why you won't fire the kerosene heaters or quarter-turn our pots or cover us with blankets, why you let this chill steal over our rows, why you drag your chair into the dim crevasse between our troughs even as your lobes and nose turn a new color, your whole face florid from the horror as hoarfrost tiptoes inside to nibble on our nodes, and Mister George Eastman once told me to *embrace light, admire it, love it, but above all, know light ...*

THANKSGIVING, SUNSET

One boy down. Another in jail. Jessica, the neighbor's fat
basset, rifles through my overturned trash cans and emerges,
clamps a turkey carcass. The dog shambles down the street's
yellow line, slides the day's zipper closed, disappears into
the cleavage of darkness at the dead end. A power easement
burrs with a blue intensity of propane torches and sacrificial steel.
Where's the body? detectives ask. A girl points toward the woods,
and the cops aren't surprised. The last of autumn departs; leaves

clench their fists, disintegrate, and the flecks dab my driveway.
These hopeless pastorals. Shit happens in suburban shadows,
subdivisions built atop haunted fields and gone farms, spots
where kids get up to trouble in carports and two-flat firetraps.
The gloaming's fire fades to the sailor's delight, and a bullet
shatters the back window. Jessica heads home.

RETURN

> *The chorus points to a secret law.*
> —Ludwig Wittgenstein on Johann Wolfgang von Goethe's *Morphology*

Down the block, a police siren belches
warning yawps. I drag to the window,
and the blue patrol car's lights strobe,
their lonely disco flashes through the hedges.
The neighborhood owls arrive.

Above my head, they hoot under soft stars.
Their alarm rises: *Ya-woo, ya-wooooo!* I'm sleeping
in the spare bedroom. Your snores reach
me across the hall. Regular breaths. I punch
the cold pillow pile, the empty side.

In the devastated elm above my window,
the loud owls mate or fight for territory—
I can't tell which. Your body, shaped
like a delicate tangle of threads, shifts.
In your window, an orange slice of moon,

a lopsided star field. The lights of a plane
blink. The air's sticky with summer's
residue. And the raptors thrash and thrash
in parched trees, hoot their maniacal mirth
as they travel away. Somewhere in the woods,

the male owl, my guide in thorough darkness,
calls, *Who cooks? Who cooks for you ALL?*

IF ONLY I COULD CHOOSE MY OWN COUNTRY,

it could be anywhere with the smell of soil as it travels
on a late-summer breeze, the sad calls of crows, the carks
from that myrtle tree as they launch into the clouds.

Down the street, a nail gun attacks something hard; a hammer
bangs. Across the lake toward the freeway, I spot a silver
flash of some sail's fabric. I wish I could follow those orange

butterflies, find a better country, go where I am no longer
skin, but a part of something flying, disappearing in forest,
in azure dark to the treed mountains where an entire curtain

of monarchs lifts, where I might find all those *Lepidoptera*
at home. It's something to admire. Their futility. Soft wings.
Fragility countered with blind persistence. I'm obsessed with it.

When I was a kid, a swarm of these butterflies, mid-route
on their flights, migrating home to Mexico, invaded my schoolyard;
thousands and thousands descended around and onto us.

They settled on our small arms,   legs,   eyebrows   in a slow flutter   coat.
Now I think of how, at this moment,
        they fill a jungle   somewhere,   and wait
    for passage north,
             for seeds
                  and to molt,
                      chrysalides,
                            and they cling to one another.
Dusty bristle legs   Velcro on and off
their fastenings. Their columns
               climb.
                      Unsettled
                            settled.
     And then their flicker bridges shake;

                                             they fly,
                                                unmoored,
                                       only cirrus
                     and no borders, just
                  arduous tasks of recreation and relocation. Every season.
            Like Sisyphus.
      Only prettier.

THE LIVES I SAVE ARE NEVER MY OWN

It's futile to rescue this semi-feral kitten who's more teenage
gawkiness than lithe adult. She's fetched a lizard and brought

it inside, and I can't find it under the couch, but the reptile's tail
has detached—a tricky distraction for predators. The separated

appendage flails on the carpet, hopscotching across the Oriental
pattern. It's a soulless, lonely thing. I often think about a stranger

I helped—if he made it home or to the hospital, if he still breathes.
It was the hottest summer on record in New York City.

In the diner where I worked, I watched weathermen on TV
fry steaks on the sidewalk. One morning during rush hour,

on my way home from the early shift, a man collapsed in front
of me on 57th Street. Unconscious, he splayed out crucifixion-style.

People circled around, gathered on the sidewalk for a spectacle.
I knew this was a heart attack, stepped forward, knelt beside him,

loosened his collar. I dipped my open lips down to his dry mouth,
his breath like a bagel. I counted kisses, breathed into his maw.

My eyes focused on his yellow tie's polka dots, calculated my air bubbles
to the circle patterns. I beat his chest in 4/4 time, *one-two-three-four,*

one-two-three-four. Air bubbles. Circle patterns. Life or something.
And when he finally coughed up froth, his eyelids twitched open

with the confused expression of a wild animal displaced. He foraged
my young face for answers. I had none. I re-fluffed his pocket square,

and the crowd clapped, and I was myself again. I scurried away,
embarrassed by my sweat-doused uniform, by all the attention,

hurried to make the train so I could change for my day job.
An ambulance siren's keening softened to a moan as I descended

the stairs into the urine-dank station. Soon after, I moved away.
Today, as the stray cat drinks from a water bowl, her back against

the wall, I guess she's stowed a litter somewhere, and I think about
that man. Now, the feline's eyes, black-rimmed and wary, dart up

with suspicion, her gaze catches on mine, and all is still in that moment
when we gaze into each other, understand as two species

might comprehend one another. She paws at the front door,
wants no part of my safe world, and I crack the exit. Florida's

humidity vines around my bare legs as the cat nudges through
the opening, then sprints like hell back to her own hot place.

A NEWSPAPER HEADLINE ANNOUNCES THAT THE BIG BANG CREATED A MIRROR UNIVERSE WHERE TIME GOES BACKWARD

That universe spins a counter-reflection, and the big bang is an implosion.
    It folds itself like an old calico whose spots dissolve, whose legs curl up,
        and it is now a fetus, now nothingness. That place's story ends with birth
            as the grand finale. Landscapes swizzle, contracting to a single cell.

        Jungles proliferate toward drought. Hard-shelled bugs and crimson
    berries appear fully formed. At launch time, atomic dust balloons already
exist. And the tape rewinds past vacuums and epochs to the start of our
rigmarole, to a woman's tombstone forgotten in a cemetery corner, to an empty

chair left in a field in desolate winter's fawn, to the corn nubs, to that old woman
    now breathing in the chair in that bare pasture, to an adolescent who now sees
        loneliness back away, to the fecund meadow with its rows of corn that ungrow
            to no meadow at all. To a clock unticking. To a car as it travels in reverse,

        unslamming into a dog in an intersection. The dog now shrinks to a puppy
    who's born wet, wriggling. Once outside the dark birth canal, chronology
corrects, and the scents of childhood reel by. Sleep progresses to bunk beds,
futons, pillow tops, California kings, to no rest, no peace, to unrequited love,

to failed appliances, bounced checks, probate. This is our universe predictably
    spinning in the correct direction. On-time, life emerges from ancient seeds
        sowed on the woman's ancestral property. Clockwise, she measures stints
            by sun shadows, bemoans her degraded body parts, elbows and knees

        creaking with age. She rests in a decrepit chair in a field and admires
    the patchworked green furrows, sits a spell, takes comfort in believing,
then collapses in the dirt. They haul her away, neglecting to remove
the weather-worn chair left empty out there.

INAUGURAL POEM, JANUARY 20, 2001

No poet was asked to read at George W. Bush's two inaugurations.

1.
What's next? I wonder,
as I know this morning
will change the course of things,
like a dam breaking
off the Mississippi
and swallowing whole towns,
only dolls and broomsticks
floating downstream,
people sitting on roof points
waiting for helicopters
to drop a line.

2.
In 2000, Atlanta's gorilla,
Willie B., died. I remember
getting fired that morning,
it was record cold as I waited
in the parking lot for my boss
to cut my last check. That day
my childhood died, somehow, too.
All my life, I'd seen Willie B.—
on grammar school field trips,
family picnics, second grade
birthday parties, when out-of-town
relatives came to visit.
An old gorilla, he'd been captive
for forty-odd years,
since he was pulled
from his mother's arms
at two or three, while his family
sat on some African hilltop,

surrounded by brown grass.
They crated him like a piece
of furniture or an artifact
from Tut's tomb, caged him
in a glass viewing room,
like those gorillas in Samsonite
commercials from the Seventies.

For humane purposes,
later, zookeepers moved Willie B.
to some forest environment
where, as the main attraction,
he squatted, the sheen of his silver
back iridescent in the noon sun,
and he chewed on leaves,
swatting mosquitoes,
surrounded by berms and fences.
His corner of the zoo, "all-natural,"
as public relations touted,
built so old Willie
could copulate in comfort.
Now, his offspring only knows
the confines of some zoo in Georgia.
His offspring has a lot to look forward to.

3.
I dreamt about the last passenger pigeon, Martha.
Last night, I heard her mentioned on TV
and looked her up on some search engine—
altavista, lycos, goto, hotbot, yahoo,
dodo, Asian elephant, rainforest,
rhino, manatee, wolf, buffalo.
I can't keep the sadness at bay,
the idea of how all those birds vanished,
how it would feel to be the last of some species.
To be mateless, incapable of continuing.

Martha, the last passenger pigeon,
died in the Cincinnati Zoo.
It was 1914.
They found her corpse
stiff on the tile floor,
her ruby eyes staring at nothing,
waiting for the taxidermist's knife.
All her kin, billions of them,
once, the most numerous bird
species on the planet,
who'd dimmed the sun
with their massive flocks,
shot down in millions,
by Gatling guns
and hunting parties,
killed for their meat,
for sport.

4.
Tonight, I look up, praying
for stars, and there aren't any.
Light pollution hides them.
Artificial daylight, so we can drive,
so we can see to get to jobs
and shopping malls,
obscures the beauty
up there, somewhere,
hidden behind the manmade light
deflecting off a ceiling
of purple and crimson clouds,
obliterating the moon's carcass,
blankets of pollution pressing down.
Through the clearing,
the moist, red clay glistens.
The trees are gone from clear-cutting.
The lights of the city
twinkle at a distance.
Through all that glimmering,

distant, some of those lights
illuminate some evil crime, some
killing, some pain that some man feels.

PROOF THROUGH THE NIGHT

It used to be an easy job. Down in the bowels of the basement, you'd watch video monitors in your security cubicle. No windows, an ergonomic chair. Radios with dials crackled with phantom voices along the wall, apprising you of changes behind the pointed iron fences, pedestrians on the mown grounds. In the corner, a cabinet for Old Glory, a crisp flag you lowered every sunset, unfurled every sunrise. As part of your duties back then, it wasn't difficult. You hoisted the flag full or half—there was no in-between. It was a task on a long checklist of to-dos. In the morning, you could mark an X and move on. At the end of the day, another X when you and a fellow guard went through the routine, raising the flag for a moment to its topmost again before it came home to you. You'd fold with your partner in a dosey-doe dance, transforming the swath of colors into a triangular pillow of importance. Half-staff doesn't make sense to you. You've never understood halfway anyway; a person's dead, or she's not. But now that big flag's always in motion. You raise and lower it often during daytime hours whenever the proclamations come down. And you run up to the roof so often it's easier for you to work from a makeshift office in the stairway landing, midway up from the bottom floor. You don't go to lunch—you call out for pizza so you can stay put. A church, a school, a movie theater. People somewhere else, living somewhere lives, then suddenly not living their somewhere lives. Maybe tomorrow,
maybe Friday. Today.
You get the call;
the order comes.
A nightclub in California.
A responder and almost
a dozen kids. Twelve people.
Twelve months. Thirteen
stripes. Fifty stars. Fifty
steps, you walk to the roof
to find the November air
churning. The flag's
metal clips *tick-tick-tickety*
against the steel pole
like a drummer's high
hat with no backbeat.
With your calloused hands,
you unwind the rough
halyard off its cleat, tug
the rope, raise it
on the pole to its peak
for an instant.

THE WORLD WILL BLOW

An aggressive vine eats its way across the South. It devours parking lots, clawing through Florida all the way to the Lake Fairy Inn's foundations. Tendrils weave along the motel's rusted railings, its rotted jambs. Creepers crawl through cracks, coming inside, taking over Ben's brain.   In these conditions, he gets angry, his plans can't flourish: whistleblowers blow their whistles, ex-girlfriends call 24-hour tip lines, and blood spills are tough to clean. Yeah, bleach only works sometimes. And DNA doesn't lie. Inside the inn's mini-fridge, a human head props on a paper plate. Behind the motel, the cricket hum's silent where the body's disappeared.   If only people didn't look through him, he wouldn't play. He builds a soul from parts, all those circuits and shrapnel.   And today, the bank's a trap. *Tick tick tick.* Ben's mechanical heartbeat thumps in a safe deposit box, jiggling double locks. Down in that basement vault, a bomb squad palms the loose cash into their Kevlar, then sweats it out as they try to disarm a complicated device. Needle-nose pliers. Tweezers. Angled dikes. Red wire. Black wire. Boom.

GHAZAL FOR A DISPIRITED PLACE

> *The wild animals seemed less predatory to him than people he had known.*
> —Marjorie Kinnan Rawlings

A black cat slinks past, stretches its spine in Florida.
A sunset spins cloud curses of purple carmine in Florida.

I hopscotch sidewalks, sweat streets, land cracks, break
my mother's back, never cross the line or win Florida.

Crowds of crows slash sleeves, caw black warnings,
carom through copses; the flock's outline trims Florida.

On a bridge railing, a gull balances, tarsus tucked tight.
A bad-luck gale rattles height-clearance signs, spins "Florida."

Next door, roofers staple-gun shingles. *Dash-dash-dash.*
Dot. Dot. Dot. Blue thunder, lightning tines, din, Florida.

Alligators yawn on the shore, bob in the rough shallows.
Skinks hiss across the sugar-sand, serpentine-sinned Florida.

Trouble's coming—*Caty, bar the door!* Pink spoonbills, blushing
feathers back-lit, beat wings, coast high to careen in Florida.

LESSON PLAN

Black crows traverse
the bunched-up sky,
nimbostratus clouds

like scratched-through
pencil marks, and an osprey
mother dances around

atop the telephone pole
where she built her nest.
She pricks across

on talon tips, shifting
her weight in the twigs
and debris with her pneumatic

march. The hatchlings
are days away from fledging—
still smallish, all flapping

wings and fluster. I turn up
the car radio as some somber-
voiced DJ reads every name

of the 49 who perished.
More folks are dead today.
Shot-gunned journalists.

Nothing's changed. I try
to concentrate, plan
explanations for freshmen

students about what our
poet of the day means when
she says, *It is June. I am tired*

of being brave. The light turns
green, but I don't see it.
Behind me, the driver

lays on her horn.
I jump off my clutch
and stall the car.

The loud report also spooks
the crows up there,
and they scatter toward

the pines. The mother
osprey lifts off, too,
abandoning her young

birds in their nest of sharp
sticks, their beaks still
kissing the sky hello.

CHYRONS RUN THROUGH MY HEAD 2

more's the pity
    to pine for death
for doses of dirt
for so much for mirth

regret tastes strange
    lavished in hurt
reserve this feat
for so much to brood

god needs to be pretty
just like you

wounded like the wind
    for a new-fangled invention
whipped like a tail
let it spew

god needs to be pretty,
    needs to be needed
just like you

we watched you jump-intrude,
    why dawn, then   when
the world didn't need news
or smudged dark floors
some unmarked minds
lost   in moments, lost and blind

tree limbs noosed   hair and eyes
    chose the tangle to see
mingled surprise
thick ropes slap in stiff breezes
those scare tactics
those heebie-jeebies

god needs to be pretty,
    needs to be
just like me

IV

DARK KNOTS

Our consonants tilled the dry fields
with trenches and then furrowed hope,
and when we screamed, when they mourned,
we all placed pebbles on an old tombstone.

Out on the pitch, a vixen carried her kits,
so stealthy, those silhouettes, black, knotted
like unblown roses. I dreamt we slept. We
didn't. At two o'clock, the coroner arrived.

PREDICAMENT

On Helen Frankenthaler's Situation

I study her extensive landscape—
    untreated canvas,
orchidacity, fluid brushstrokes,
    the striations
an explosion, geology bombs.
Predicaments.
The palette's plates
tremor. Seismic
    gashes, faded geodes
a chiaroscuro line, quake
toward citrine & dabbed amethyst
trembling atop lapis lazuli.

With my forefinger, I poke
at the protruded slope, its toe
a hood rendered with imprecision,
    scraped across raw
    linen where the artist's
fault lines cave, lose confidence.

I delight in this crime, this touching;
    I lean in & purse my wet lips
to kiss the dry surface. I lick
    her taut fabric.
    The painting springs back,
salty & needy. Alone.

For my misconduct,
    I await some alarm,
    some stern guard or peeved
patron, but like Frankenthaler's
    Situation, I'm ignored
in this corner of the Speed,
    unseen under a red
emergency-exit sign, invisible
as I flutter my stupid tongue.

IN MARGHERITA'S KINGDOM, A VILLANELLE

After the photograph by Mario Lasalandra (1967)

Here, what cheer? The sorceress hears of hills that grow books.
Jigs and rhymes—saddle-shoe lost time. Bleached crinolines,
a photo's chockablock hole shots, faint letters pop-locked, unshook.

Here, she spells sin, curses cliffs, bans noisome nooks,
spindrifts brine, that gray grind, the old tides' boss.
Hear, what cheer, the sorceress hears of hills that grow books.

There, a hedge cloud. A noon shadow falls, hears no hook.
Ring bells, carillons on-the-brook. Toll, tarot sorceress,
a photo's chockablock, hole shots feint, letters pop-locked. Unshook.

Here, she spiders cobwebs, quivers maps, witch silk unspooked.
Hear spooled jetties, tidepools, tadpoles that churn and toss
here. What cheer, the sorceress hears of hills that grow books.

Hear tall tales she tells, spills such terms, such sorcery cooks.
Here, rhymes aperture, don f-stop chokers, le juju albatross.
A photo's chock. A block hole. Shots feint letters, pop, lock. Done shook.

Hear libraries spout gibberish, all manner of gobbledygook.
See. Have a look. There, there, tossed contrappostos criss-cross
here. What cheer the sorceress hears! Of hills that grow, books.
A photo's chockablock. Hole shots faint letters. Pop-lock dun's hook.

SHORTEST COMPLETE SENTENCE IN THE ENGLISH LANGUAGE
A CENTO

Here eucalyptus,
        cedar shadow,
                dreams.
I shall be called a wife to pattern by,
with a watchful and elegant mind.

                        Leaves dandle
names of trees and flowers and weeds
and add some extra, just for you.
        As if before dark,
they fill you with the faults they had.

At least one kind of traditional magic:
open this picture and find anything
                redundant but syncopated.
Muddy streams keep him fixed for good.

Slowly light strengthens, and the room takes shape.
How many constants *should* there be?
Your own six senses
    sing sin. We
                net
      seven at the Golden Shovel.
Work has to be done.

And some day when you knock and push the door,
& then love the human: wives   husbands   and friends,
breathing
        dead reckoning's
                song,
        I never again shall tell you what I think.
        No.

QUIET MOMENTS DESERVE HEROES

Gustave Courbet contemplates his painting Still Life with Apples and Pomegranate

1.
The hues speak for me—red
    and right,
        subterranean wet
blue,
    Devil-may-care viridian.
I practice, aim to interpret
    all that fruit
        in a bowl.

A peck of apples, a lonely
    pomegranate, the smudged
        glass, pewter jug.
Another dab of ochre
or emerald with less cadmium
yellow, more umber to stalk
        shadows on the bowl.
Quiet moments deserve heroes.

2.
My vignette darkens in the late
afternoon, and the window loses
its battle to the dark. Finally,
when the shadows shift,
    I stop, sign my name
        with an exclamation point,
    punctuate my work with a dot
and dash to mark the end.
Like an emergency.

When I pack my easel into gangly
    angles and hang my moist
        canvas on a hook,
swish turpentine through

    my brushes, tap them dry,
    I know it's not over.

Even now, with my indelible
vision that exists for all to see,
it's still a still-life with the oil paint
    tacky to the touch
years after a piece is complete.

I envy paintings' endings,
their outcomes recorded
in dollops on linen,
    facsimiles that never fade like life.

3.
Apples. I imagine
last spring's orchards,
how bees hummed
    and voluted, dusted
        flower to white flower,
        the buds' bursting
later that summer.

4.
I'll be away
for weeks, yet I choose not to
clear away this fruit or fold
that rumpled velvet on the
assemblage's table.
I face the artificial configuration
and reckon a new array
will soon emerge—early autumn
will breathe warmth
    onto the squat terracotta
    container, and the fruit
    will withdraw its touch,

    incarnadine skin will shrivel
        back by degrees, a foreskin
            retracting, the peel
            shrinking away
            to russet husks.

5.
These wares will sit
alone through days of quiet;
in an empty room,
a slow pouring of bitumen
        black. The gloom's lavender
fingers will grab
away the tartness and caress
        the glaucous flesh.
And the flies. They'll pick at
        the apples' powder
of mold, nest in the slime,
        in the creases of rot.

6.
Though all things wither,
        I push to the end.
I know the future of these
lowly objects, the small-scale
ripeness, temporary,
how the sun chiaroscuros
corners, battles more impressive
than any sword fight.

Wine turns. Still, life,
        in all its small
        hours, arrives.
        As I leave my studio,
I pick my snack, half-green,
        so firm, from the bottom
            of the pile,
and rub it on my smock
so it shines.

HUNTERS & COLLECTORS

A kind of funeral at the science center.
I press a button, & it comes alive;
the recessed fixtures flicker in the ceiling.
Up close, an ax-cut cypress,
a fake trunk. Swamp light soughs shadows,

crepuscular light. Cricket sounds from hidden
speakers stridulate, a brown pointillist
rustle through bendable trees.
Spiderweb, butterfly, bee.
Autumnal redolence wafts along the floor.

That smell. I'm transported to the creek
where I played as a kid.
On the bank, veiled
with gnats, I fashioned
a fort of collapsing sticks,
hid my treasures under pine straw:
translucent beetle husks,
white-green lichen lace,
& pink quartz.
Precious gems caked with orange clay.

Back here at this museum, I follow a white
cottontail as it disappears
into a culvert.
Rotting leaves & larvae
squiggle & twirl question marks in a resined pond.
Two foxes have eaten the rabbit's
mate, strewn its fur
across the diorama.
A cemetery in the woods.
A second rabbit escapes into a copse
as the painted nightscape blinks beyond.

Those foxes. They lounge
like royalty. The female rests
her paw
on her prey's remains
as if patting it to sleep. Her amber eyes
all taxidermy shine
& weary frankness.

A child crosses the gallery, drawn
to the drama. The girl's wet nose pokes
at the glass. *What are the foxes doing?* she asks.
Her mother checks her watch.
The father taps
his daughter's shoulder. *They killed it. For food.*
The kid's mouth opens, closes,
her soft baby teeth pointed.

CONSEQUENCES IN WATER

For all of us who dread the dim light, who stare
at the stars for understanding, whose eyes adjust
    at dusk, our perfect mammal smallness

is a pressure. Yesterday, I screamed at my own
inconsequence. My guttural yell rifled like gunshots.
    It reached nothing, unlike the ocean's

prompts, touching wherever they go. On tribal
islands, washerwomen scrub laundry on the breakwater
    rocks. Some men canoe to an isthmus

for the best catch. And through spume barrels,
a child stands on a board and ducks. Most people
    don't question, but pay tributes to the sea's

foam thudding their shores, the water's high-tide
petticoats that sift all kinds of sky-sun-cloud-airplane
    reflections. I wish I could read those scribblings

on the surface or tonight's half-moon that tugs at me.
Blue driftwood, striped with salt, piles itself onshore.
    And right now, sails of shadow—cumulonimbus

fleets, armadas of stars—move over all the fish and their
crazy calligraphy language. I look upward and spy the ink
    smudges of bat wings going everywhere. Nowhere.

INEFFABLE

After Seamus Heaney's "Postscript"

Storms uncurl their cloud-to-ocean
    ribbons, forked lightning. The blinks
        score dark acreages of the sea. Thunder slaps
            the distance, smacks the rutted
    waves, & dissolves. Flicked foam
flocks the spit. The high tide obsidians.

But I know nothing swims in certainty. Even
    a construction of cranes will burst into flight,
        their gray-on-gray wings bobbin to a smudge
            in the pitch-white lid. A drizzle veils
        that small flock as they strafe the purring pickups
on the road's shoulder. Those birds keep going & sail

the cirrus jibs. When this wind & light
    work on each other, I struggle to make
        firsts, not seconds. Air-to-earth lightning
scores a swath of sea. The dead no-sound flashes across guttural
    silence; the cove slip's green-blue blackens. Squalls call, foam
        & froth the surface. Some sandhill cranes beat the gusts, tough
tussling. Red on gray on white. They dodge dump trucks on the freeway, rejiggering
    their flight. There, where my enjambments, my lines, rhymes fall on this rainy day,
                                      I come about, glide through the grief.

RESURFACE

My appetite for flowers & easy light. For woodlands
Amniotic, unkempt. The wildest things are most alive.
Fallen trees & their branches, tangled brush & brambles thrive.
All sprawl. No clean footpath or trail to cut. When I quicksand,

Sucked past the forest's high-water mark, a dull pain floats
Up. Stitched fingers, clammy palms. Threaded nettle hyacinths,
Thorns, spines & stings of noontime, the sun-mote spray. Labyrinth,
Pricks of time ticking on the shore's soft placket. Those boats,

Such small boats. No sails, no masts. The light pisses splinters.
The swamp spits me out, a tough escape from these haunted bogs.
Only stories, such imprecise words, strew through earnest slogs,
Blinked-out moments below. If I resurface, disinter,

I have lived in this canvas, in this frightening frontier.
Nothing's discouraged me. I shouldn't exist, yet I'm here.

THE LOON WAILS THIS MORNING

The loon wails this morning about mysteries
and clarion songs, a world bedecked. Soon,

her cries will bevel away, fade as she crosses the lake.
But now, she drifts and bobs and demands.

Under her hull, below the water, I'm sure that fowl
furiously paddles in cut-time. The surface, such

velvety liquid, ruches as her boat skirts its navigation
lane. I study her treading the cold current. I can only spot

her craft as it glides forth. I can't see her webbed feet
work. I can't see anything inside myself. Everything here

seals, everything's shut like a ship's cabinet—airtight,
yet packed with a jumble of potions and pots.

We're corpuscles and kidneys, sweat and shit and spit,
admixtures, fragile parts in fancy wrappings. Veined limbs.

Iridescent feathers. Out there in the deep, in the dawn,
that loon accepts neither silence nor uncertainty. Her keening

forms a search party, the trumpets tremolo through the fog
to reach a cove's copse of sweetgums. The trees hug

a soon-bright bank, and her mate waits in the shallows.
He soft yodels a response. Of course, I only imagine those

creatures' intentions. Who knows what happens? I won't ever
wander into that inlet far in the distance, never map its interiors,

but I can prick up my ears and listen for signals I'll never fathom.

QUIET OBSERVATION, DECAY, & THE VIOLENCE SIMMERING UNDER THE SURFACE OF THE ORDINARY
A CONVERSATION BETWEEN CATE MCGOWAN & SARA MOORE WAGNER

Cate, I am so glad to have acquired this book as an Editors' Prize pick. I loved it deeply, from my very first read. Because we read anonymously at *Driftwood*, I only learned about your success in other genres when your name and cover letter were revealed. Tell me about your journey through the genres that has led you to this book.

Thank you, Sara—your choosing my book is such a huge honor. *Driftwood* is my dream press!

I've often contended with opposing impulses, my writing journey an organic evolution of form and content—a migration that feels almost as natural as aging. My first forays into writing were actually in poetry. As a very young writer, I found myself captivated by the way language can distill emotion and experience into sharp bursts of imagery. I asked for Robert Frost's collected poems for my twelfth birthday and devoured that book. I was also obsessed with Carl Sandburg's poem "Fog," Elizabeth Barrett Browning's sonnets, and Edgar Lee Masters' *Spoon River Anthology*. Those books are still on my shelf.

But, like many, I figured if I wanted success, I should write stories. My family always said I could keep everyone entertained with my tales, and I loved writing scholarly essays in college. So, prose somehow seemed like the way to go. I shifted to fiction, immersing myself in devising narratives, though I always infused anything I wrote with lyricism, falling in love with the sounds of phrases or the image of something that was sometimes *very* beside the point.

While I've been fortunate to publish three prose books—a story collection, a novel, and a collection of essays—none are bestsellers. And I've always had a nagging sense that I wasn't fully expressing myself as a writer. I realized at some point that if I wanted to share my deepest self, I needed to stop avoiding the poems I knew I had in me. But the shift wasn't just about coming to terms with poetry; there was a reckoning with what others expected. A person in my immediate circle, a romance novelist, once told me that my literary fiction is pointless—they stressed how their genre keeps the financial wheels of the literary world turning. They were right, of course, but I was devastated by this person's cruelty—and the realization. I don't see romance novels as art. Sure, they're a kick, but they don't ask the big questions I think literature should ask, and they don't push boundaries. They're formulaic, driven by tropes to entertain or titillate. I don't want to write plug-and-play stories.

For me, literature has always been about more than that. I care about the conditions of our world, humanity, and nature. With its concision and intensity, poetry is a medium where I can address these more profound questions more directly. I've come to accept that I won't be successful by society's standards—no bestsellers, no sweeping romances—but I'm at peace with writing what I want, how I want, and trying to answer the questions that matter most to me. That's what led me back to poetry and this collection, where I can create art that speaks to the complexities of life.

I think that might be another reason why we're a perfect match! At *Driftwood*, our top priority is art and craft. It's so clear to me that this book puts the impulse towards aesthetics first. There is quite a bit of ekphrasis here—what is the role of art in your poems? What kind of art most inspires you?

Art serves as both a mirror and portal in my work, reflecting the world as I see it while opening new ways to perceive it. I've always been deeply connected to art—it runs through my family. My grandmother was a professional artist, as was one of her brothers. My sister's a designer; my brother looks at the world through a 3D filter. A sculptor in the best way.

As a child, I fell asleep every night gazing down the hallway at her paintings on our walls. She was an incredible portraitist and landscape painter. I've worn many artistic hats, including working as a professional calligrapher and textile designer. I was supposed to attend art school, but life got in the way. I worked as a gallerista for years and finally became an art historian—I write about art, but I'm art adjacent. I paint and draw as a hobbyist, but I don't think I'm good enough to make a go of it. So yes, art has never been just a passion for me; it's a lifeline, a family trade, a career choice, an obsession woven into everything I've ever done.

Ekphrasis is an essential tool for me as I explore the intersections of various art forms, creating a layered dialogue between the visual and the verbal. I've always been fascinated by how a visual form can, like poetry, distill emotion, memory, and experience into something tangible.

My love for the visual arts spans hundreds of artists who inspire me, each in different ways. My happy place is writing art criticism, looking at a work and its contextual relevance. Some of my recent favorite topics are Caravaggio's dramatic chiaroscuro, Degas' intimate (and strangely feminist) portrayals of dancers, Leonora Carrington's surreal and mythic landscapes, and Hopper's meditations on isolation. Rothko's color fields move me deeply—his subtle shifts in color evoke emotional depths that words sometimes can't reach. And I also admire concrete poetry, where the physical arrangement of words becomes part of the meaning, echoing my fascination with the materiality of art itself.

These are just a few artists who inspire me, as choosing a favorite is impossible. Each offers a unique way of seeing the world, and that diversity of perspectives is something I try to bring into my work. Art and poetry are two sides of the same coin—both offer a means to explore and express the intricate, often contradictory emotions and truths that shape human experience.

The first poem in this book gestures to what can be captured in the "brevity" and "truncation" of a poem that, perhaps, is more difficult elsewhere? What makes you turn to poetry? Is there a way you know something should be a poem (rather than a painting, an essay or a story)?

Poetry demands economy of language that forces me to distill emotions into purer forms, to strip away extraneousness. I often know something should be a poem when I feel that the experience or emotion needs to be encapsulated in a discrete image or moment of visceral clarity. A poem is the compression of thought into a lyrical burst rather than the narrative arc required by fiction or the reflective expanse of an essay. Sometimes, a poem's about how much weight a moment can bear before it fractures or expands. I'm continually navigating that edge, deciding if an idea needs room to breathe or can survive under the pressure of poetic form.

Many of the poems contain braiding (in addition to the literal Samson braids in "Cuts"). You expertly weave in familiar characters like Samson, art (as mentioned), and scientific information. It feels true, what you say, that "history's crackled record/ is [yours] now." Does this sort of braiding come naturally to you? What role does research play in your writing process?

Braiding is how I process and express thought. Many of my stories are non-linear; my essays combine academic scholarship and personal anecdotes. And I've always been drawn to the complexity of interwoven narratives like they're stacked objects in a cabinet of curiosities. Perhaps my fascination also stems from my deep engagement with music, where melodies and rhythms overlap to create something more significant than the sum of their parts, something transcendent. This layering method allows me to juxtapose the personal with the historical, the sacred with the scientific, creating strata of meaning that readers can peel away. Research is the thread that holds this all together, grounding my work in the real world even as I push into the symbolic. What's research for me? My life experiences spur me to make sense of what's happened. To sort out my disasters and curiosity and to try to understand the world's little beautiful facts, I read philosophy, critical scholarship, and scientific findings written by people so much smarter than me. The more I know, the more I realize I know nothing. It's humbling and exhilarating. But my way of looking at the world isn't just about gathering facts; it's about how facts can contextualize my personal, emotional truths into something external and universal.

These poems are richly lyric, in the traditional sense. I'm very drawn to

the way you use sound. They are incredibly musical and controlled. In which stage of writing does sound come in for you? Do you have advice for poets who might want to experiment more with sound?

Sound is fundamental to my writing process—it's present from the very beginning, shaping the rhythm and movement of the poem, sometimes even before a concrete meaning emerges. I often think about one of my writing mentors who was blind, so my art references in those early poems weren't as effective at bandaging my crap. He stressed the importance of the sounds of words and made me work to create stanzas that sang.

Now, heeding words' aural effects is my primary springboard. I walk around for days repeating a line, with the rhythm or sound stuck in my head like an earworm, like a song I can't get out of my head. I do this with my fiction as well. These phrases haunt and nag at me until I sit down and complete the piece. I'm a musician with years of vocal training, and though the visual world and art are the eyes of my work, my poems' voices are crucial to conveying more profound meanings. My drummer husband often listens as I read my work aloud. He pays attention to the meter and tempo, and when he says, "That's got it," I know I've hit the right note.

For any poets interested in poetry's musicality, I suggest reading your poems aloud at every stage of the writing process. Let what you hear guide you—where does the rhythm feel natural? Where does it stumble? Play with repetition, alliteration, assonance, consonance, and unexpected word combinations. Don't be afraid to embrace music, even if it feels unconventional. Try using a form as a framework, allowing the constraints to push you toward new sonic textures. Sonnets sound different than pantoums. Embrace the difficulty! Aural effects can transform how meaning is delivered on a fundamental, primal level, often revealing subtleties and layers that the words alone might not convey.

Your use of form really does relate to this, from prose to pantoums to centos to invented forms. In an interview Diane Seuss did with Jennifer Franklin for *The Poetry Society of America*, she said, "Form is what the world is—a concept, brought into materiality. Our bodies are forms. The places where we live. The construction of a root system, or a worm." As a poet, I am drawn similarly to form, as a natural reflection of the world. What draws you to formal poetry? How do you approach a form, once you decide to write in it?

Form is easier for me than free verse. I don't know why—it's maddening. For me, a formal structure works as a discrete container with limits, so there are finite possibilities to make a poem mean something. Within these forms, I find liberation; I'm not overwhelmed with limitations, but embrace the challenge. It's the paradox of using constraint to unlock creativity. When approaching a form like a villanelle or a ghazal, I often search for the tension between structure and freedom. The form provides the boundaries, but my role is to see how far I can stretch those boundaries before they break, to see what new shapes I can make within them. It's a dance between control and surrender, a type of choreography where the steps are known, but the movements are still my own.

And like Seuss, I believe formal poetry reflects our daily structures—our bodies, relationships, and even social constraints.

The book itself, while in conversation with form, seems to defy tight restraints of things like form. It starts with many themes, taking us into the dark space of confession and different kinds of grief instantly. It feels epic and human, like everything exists at once, as it does. There are a lot of different thoughts spiraling around the literary community about ordering collections—some readers favor tighter thematic books, some think that's too easy for the complicated work of poetry. How did you approach ordering this book? Were there any books that influenced you?

Ordering this collection was a *bear*. It went through at least 500 different iterations. What I settled on was less about thematic constraints and more about creating an emotional arc reflecting the turbulent, non-linear nature of grief, identity, and survival. Life doesn't unfold in neat, thematic packages; it comes at us in waves, in spirals, and I wanted *Sacrificial Steel* to reflect that sense of fragmented totality. Each section moves between different moods and moments, from confessional to contemplative, but always grounded in a viscerality that threads throughout the collection. I was influenced by books like Claudia Rankine's *Citizen*, where form and content collide in an uncontainable way, and Brigit Pegeen Kelly's *Song*, which demonstrates how powerful lyric and image can flow into one another, creating a more profound emotional timbre that transcends structure. I wanted my collection to mirror this simultaneity, how different griefs and joys coexist without compartmentalization.

I'd love to hear more about the voices you inhabit in this collection, they feel connected to what women do within traditional, patriarchal society, the masking that happens within a marriage, and the masks that sometimes slip away.

Many of the voices in *Sacrificial Steel* speak from the margins, negotiating power and vulnerability in a world that often confines them to roles of silence and submission. As I was crafting these poems, I began to think of the female speakers as almost donning armor, kind of similar to the way you describe masks—not in the sense of a rigid defense, but as a necessary protection for survival. The armor becomes a potent symbol of how these women navigate their realities, adopting performative identities imposed by society. Some speakers wear this armor to endure their circumstances, but there are moments when the weight of silence and repression becomes too much, and the shine on that helm begins to dull and crack, revealing unfiltered truths beneath. Throughout the collection, I tried to carry this tension between protection and vulnerability, illustrating how women move between their outward roles and internal realities.

In "Mother Courage," the speaker reflects on the stifling silence of domestic life and the burdens that come with traditional roles—wife, caregiver, dutiful partner. The poem juxtaposes the quiet mundanity of the speaker's daily life with the underlying dissatisfaction simmering beneath the surface. The compliant wife wears the armor to maintain order and routine in the face of inner turmoil. But the armor has chinks. It's incomplete in moments of quiet rebellion, where the speaker's discontent and exhaustion reveal the depths of her struggles.

Similarly, "Reckoning" deals with the loss of love rather than overt power dynamics. The speaker reflects on the dissolution of a relationship, where love has quietly disintegrated, leaving behind only the remnants of a once-shared life. The poem captures that moment of recognition when both parties realize that what once connected them has disappeared. The loss is subtle but profound, and the speaker acknowledges it through small, everyday details—the neglected home, the silence, the smoke. In this context, the armor represents not just the roles we play in relationships, but also how we shield ourselves from the painful truths of emotional loss. The speaker faces the stark reality of love's absence as her armor unbuckles.

Your exploration of love and tradition, the "compliant" wife, the "roles," as you say, is one thing that really engaged me. Recently, a student casually mentioned that her mother told her that if Taylor Swift ever got married, she'd have to step back from her fame. This struck me as a sad truth in the lives of women artists who, like those historical models of astronomically talented women like Mary Shelley and Sylvia Plath, are expected to take a backseat to the ambitions of men. You and your husband are both artists—is this pressure present for you (from whatever source)? What advice do you have for women who might feel themselves stepping back in this way?

I've hit the glass ceiling so often that its shards are permanently embedded in my scalp. The expectations of women to step back and be supportive but never fully in the spotlight are engrained in so many cultural narratives—ones that I've pushed against my entire life. My deeply Catholic upbringing and the faith I eventually left behind would have deemed me a second-class citizen, expected to be subservient. Moving away at an early age, living in New York, and trying to make it as a model and actress, I quickly realized that I was viewed more as an object than a person with agency. College gave me the tools to reframe my experiences and claim my voice.

My father's death when I was nine profoundly shaped me. His absence is woven into many of these poems. I watched my mother struggle to raise three children on her own, and while I admired her strength and loved her deeply, appreciating all her sacrifices, I didn't want to repeat that life. Ironically, when I couldn't have children myself, a part of me felt almost relieved. It was as though I had been spared from the struggles I had witnessed. Yet, I pine for that connection and feel the absence of what many consider life's most precious experience. I love children, and I love teaching them, but I also recognize that not conforming to traditional roles has allowed me to forge my own path as an artist.

My advice for women artists facing similar pressures is simple: rage against it. Society will always try to confine women to particular roles, especially when balancing marriage, motherhood, and ambition. But we can write our own stories. We don't have to retreat. We are allowed to take up space, and we should demand it. It's not about rejecting tradition but reshaping it on our own terms.

Your title, *Sacrificial Steel*, comes from the poem "Thanksgiving, Sunset." I love how the poem and title both capture so much about the collection. It feels a bit like "Ozymandias," the idea of the mighty falling and then what's next, the suburbs and things we build, the violence underneath, and the observing eye—the reader, the speaker, the girl, the cops, Jessica. It's shifting and whole, like the collection! How did you decide on this as a title? Were there any other titles you cycled through?

It's almost like you're reading my mind! I really struggled with finding a title for this book. The first working title was *Clamor and Plenitude*, and then I tried *The Lives I Save Are Never My Own*, the title of one of the poems. After that, I considered *So Far, Silence*—I loved the alliteration in that. *Dead Spent* was another contender, but none of them felt right. Then, when I came across the concept of "sacrificial steel," I knew I had it.

What is "sacrificial steel"? It's an industrial method in corrosion protection known as sacrificial anode cathodic protection, where a more reactive metal, such as steel, zinc, or magnesium, is deliberately allowed to corrode in place of a more valuable structure—like a pipeline or ship—to protect it from rust. The sacrificial metal "sacrifices" itself to extend the life of the protected material.

This metaphor struck me as a perfect representation of the collection's central themes—the often unnoticed, silent sacrifices people make to protect what is fragile. Throughout the book, and especially in "Thanksgiving, Sunset," this idea manifests. Individuals endure suffering and decay, whether it's to protect a family, preserve a culture, or shield something dear from harm. Much like the steel that sacrifices itself to corrosion, these sacrifices often go unseen but are crucial for preserving something greater.

The title also speaks to the tension between strength and vulnerability throughout the collection. Steel, which we associate with power and endurance, is still subject to corrosion and breaking under pressure. This duality—of resilience and fragility—captures the heart of the book, as does the poem "Thanksgiving, Sunset," which compresses these ideas of quiet observation, decay, and the violence simmering under the surface of the ordinary. While I cycled through other titles that captured elements of the collection, *Sacrificial Steel* felt the most encompassing, capturing the balance of strength and vulnerability that defines the work.

I just love that concept. It's the perfect title! Domesticated and suburban animals also could fit into that concept of what's under the surface and fragile. They roam through this collection, dogs, cats, owls, crows—there are so many! The human world, in contrast, seems so much more vicious and wild (especially in poems like "Hunters & Collectors"). This makes these poems feel like ecopoetry. I've heard a lot of poets trying to define ecopoetry—what the ecopoem is or should be. How do you approach writing an environmental poem? What do you hope your most ecological poems achieve?

Yeah, I didn't sit down with a pencil and piece of paper one day and say, "Today, I shall commence composing an ecopoem." I never intended to write ecopoetry, but I guess I did, didn't I? The natural world has always been a vital part of my life. I love to go outside and play in the woods or even sit on the beach and watch the sun jangle across the waves, so these ecopoems are a natural outgrowth of my spiritual, naturalist self. Ecopoetry emphasizes our interconnectedness with the natural world, a connection that's often ignored or disrupted by human violence, consumerism, or apathy.

In my approach to writing about the environment, I aim to blur the boundaries between human and non-human worlds, making it clear that our actions—benign or destructive—are never isolated from our ecosystems. In poems like "Hunters & Collectors," I wanted to juxtapose the savagery we often attribute to animals with the more sinister violence of humans, especially in spaces where a veneer of civility frequently masks brutality. I hope these poems provoke a re-evaluation of how we view and interact with the natural world, not as something separate from us, but as an intrinsic part of our collective survival or demise.

Many of these poems also feel political, as does the book as a whole (the personal and ecological being political!), but I'm especially drawn to your "Inaugural Poem, January 20, 2001." In a tweet recently, as a seeming response to Amanda Gorman reading at the Democratic National Convention, Danez Smith said, "Make art that seeks to tear down empire,

confronts it with honesty and teeth. Don't glamorize empire, don't assist it, don't make it your muse or you will be its mule." This poem aligns with that idea of honesty and teeth exactly. Do you agree that this is the role of American poets now?**

Absolutely. In times of political unrest and ecological crisis, poets have a responsibility to engage with the world honestly, to confront the structures of power that perpetuate injustice. Poetry has always been a vehicle for dissent, and its role is especially crucial now.

Yet, like Seamus Heaney, I'm ambivalent about contributing. In his 1988 essay, "The Government of the Tongue," written during Northern Ireland's Troubles, Heaney expressed his doubts about poetry's ability to effect change. Though he affirms poetry's "unlimited" worth, he acknowledges its limitations: "The efficacy of poetry is nil—no lyric has ever stopped a tank" (p. 107). Decades earlier, Marxist playwright Bertolt Brecht echoed a similar sentiment, as Terry Eagleton recounts: Brecht noted that "putting a factory on stage would tell you nothing about the nature of capitalism" (p. 68). I share Heaney's and Brecht's concerns about the limitations of art to inspire direct political change. Representations of real life are always artificial constructions.

But still, we must try. "Inaugural Poem, January 20, 2001" was born from a place of witnessing, of personal and national upheaval. I wrote it on the day George W. Bush was inaugurated when I was distraught over the Supreme Court's decision to halt the Florida recount and hand him the presidency. It was a cold day in Atlanta, and I felt unaccomplished just before a milestone birthday. My car had broken down, and as I sat in the mechanic's parking lot in my boyfriend's pickup, I quickly jotted out that poem in about five minutes, feeling as though the world was headed for dark times. And indeed, we were. That poem, written in a moment of frustration and foreboding, became my first poetry publication—over fifteen years later, Allison Joseph took a chance on it for *Crab Orchard Review*.

So, yes, I agree with Smith. As poets, our task isn't to serve as mere commentators, but to wield our craft in ways that challenge the systems that oppress and exploit. Art can be beautiful, but it should also have teeth—it should unsettle, provoke, and force readers to confront uncomfortable truths. The political and personal are inseparable, and I hope my work reflects that necessary fusion.

It absolutely does! Thinking about American politics, the end of this book takes us to Florida in a really visceral way. Of course, Florida is a hotbed literally and politically. What is your relationship to Florida? What do you wish readers would take away about this place?

Florida's a place of contradictions—lush and deadly, full of beauty and decay. It's a state where nature seems to exist on the edge of chaos and where humans mirror that precarity. My relationship with Florida is one of deep ambivalence—I've lived here for a while, but it's never felt like home. Sure, it's a place that's shaped me, but I've often wanted to escape, especially in the last few years.

In *Sacrificial Steel,* Florida becomes a backdrop for personal and collective unraveling, a landscape where the human-made and the natural world collide in often disastrous ways. I hope readers come away with a sense of Florida's complexity—a place where beauty and brutality coexist, where the environment witnesses and participates in the cycles of personal and political destruction and regeneration that define contemporary life.

How will you approach your next collection of poetry? Do you, perhaps, have the next project in mind? What's next for you in the other genres you work in?

I almost have another complete collection ready to go, all orphan poems—they're pieces that didn't quite fit the themes or vibe of *Sacrificial Steel*. But I haven't abandoned those poor dears; I'm working on a new collection where those poems might find a home as I try to discover a connective thread. I've also just completed another collection of short stories, leaning on Todorov's theory of the fantastic. I'm drawn to how the fantastic disrupts reality, creating moments of cognitive dissonance, and I've been exploring that tension in my fiction.

Additionally, I've been slowly writing an auto-novel about growing up in Atlanta during the Missing and Murdered Children crisis. It's a story that's haunted me for years, and I feel an urgency to address the racism and misogyny I witnessed during that era (and continue to see). It's a narrative where personal history meets collective trauma, and I hope to amplify often silenced or overlooked voices.

Beyond poetry and fiction, I'm also working on essays, though creative nonfiction tends to unnerve me more than the other genres. In fiction and sometimes in poetry, there's a layer of distance between me and the truths I explore, a space to shape the narrative more freely. But in essays, there's no filter—what I'm writing about is my direct experience, my own truths—and that vulnerability can be overwhelming. Still, I've found that it's in those raw moments where some of my most powerful writing emerges.

Whether I'm working in poetry, fiction, or nonfiction, all my projects share a common thread: they're driven by a deep pursuit of veracity and an exploration of life's complex, sometimes painful realities. Each genre allows me to approach truths from a different angle, but the aim remains the same.

References

Eagleton, T. (2013). *The gatekeeper: A memoir.* St. Martin's Press.

Heaney, S. (1988). The government of the tongue. In The government of the tongue (pp. 91–108). *Faber and Faber.*

NOTES

Page 5, "Cuts":
The story of Samson and Delilah is a biblical tale in which the mighty Samson, endowed with superhuman strength, falls in love with Delilah, who ultimately betrays him by discovering and revealing that his strength lies in his uncut hair. Delilah's treachery leads to Samson's capture by the Philistines, who blind and enslave him.

Page 10, "Falling is the Deadest Thing":
Lines borrowed:
    Line 1 "Water" by Anne Sexton
    Line 2 "Nothingness" by Dawn Lundy Martin
    Lines 7 and 25 "Summer Near the River" by Carolyn Kizer
    Lines 3 and 17 "Those Winter Sundays" By Robert Hayden
    Lines 4 and 15 "Variation on a Theme" by W. S. Merwin
    Lines 5 and 26 "Leaving Another Kingdom" by Gerald Stern
    Line 6 "Ritual for Ash" by Cindy Williams Gutiérrez
    Lines 13 and 24 "Digging" By Seamus Heaney
    Lines 9 and 16 "Skin Canoes" by Carolyn Forché
    Line 10 "Water Calligraphy" by Arthur Sze
    Line 11 from "Coda to History: It Is Not As If" by Kwame Dawes
    Line 12 "Water, Winter, Fire" by Marvin Bell
    Line 14 "Water, Stone, Wind" by Octavio Paz
    Line 18 "Neutral Tones" by Thomas Hardy
    Line 19 and 21 "Love Letter (Clouds)" by Sarah Mangusso
    Line 20 "You, Therefore" by Reginald Shepherd
    Line 22 "Lines Depicting Simple Happiness" by Peter Gizzi
    Line 23 "Say Water" by Rad Smith

Page 12, "The Sympathy of Clocks":
The sympathy of clocks is a phenomenon observed when two or more pendulum clocks placed in close proximity to one another begin to synchronize their movements over time. This synchronization occurs because subtle vibrations transmit through a shared surface or medium, and the clocks gradually align their swinging in unison.

Page 18, "Dance This Mess Around":
"Dance This Mess Around" is a song by the B-52s. Other lyrics by the Ramones and Hall and Oates.

Page 27, "Every Body Has Ghosts":
Storeria dekayi, commonly known as the De Kay's brown snake, is a small garden serpent found in wet leaves and shade and is native to North and Central America.

Page 39, "Embrace light, admire it, love it":
The quote, "Embrace light, admire it, love it—but above all, know light," is attributed to George Eastman, industrial magnate and founder of the Eastman-Kodak Company.

Page 66, "Predicament":
Helen Frankenthaler's acrylic on canvas painting, *Situation* (1965; 51 3/8 × 120 1/4 × 3/4 in), housed at the Speed Art Museum in Louisville, Kentucky, is a striking example of color-field painting. Using her signature soak-stain technique, Frankenthaler's pigments bleed into the unprimed canvas.

Page 67, "In Margherita's Kingdom, A Villanelle":
The first three words in William Shakespeare's *The Tempest* are "Here, what cheer?"

Page 68, "Shortest Complete Sentence in the English Language":
Lines borrowed:
- Lines 1, 6, 9, 13, 16, 19, 24, and 26 "Native" by Rae Armentraut
- Lines 2, 23, and 25 "Sweat Song" by Rae Armentraut
- Lines 3, 5, 7, 11, 17, and 21 "What You Should Know to Be a Poet" by Gary Snyder
- Lines 4, 22, and 26 "Oh, Oh, You Will Be Sorry for that Word" by Gary Snyder
- Lines 8, 10, 12 "This Be the Verse" by Philip Larkin
- Title and lines 18 and 20 "We Real Cool" by Gwendolyn Brooks
- Line 14 "Riverbank Blues" by Sterling A. Brown
- Lines 15 and 21 "Aubade" Philip Larkin

ACKNOWLEDGEMENTS

"Catechism or Parting Pantoum," *Susurrus*, 2023
"Consequences in Water," *Birdcoat Quarterly*, 2020
"Cuts," *Citron Review*, 2021
"Chyrons Run Through My Head," *5th Wall*, 2018
"Dark Knots," *Rogue Agent*, 2019
"Depending on the Horizon," *Unbroken Journal*, 2018
"Embrace light, admire it, love it," *Hypertext Magazine*, 2021
"Every Body Has Ghosts," *Luna Luna Magazine*, 2020
"Falling Is the Deadest Thing," *Citron Review*, 2021
"Fold the Shadows," *Chestnut Quarterly*, 2022
"For My Mother, Who Is Dead, But Spent Too Long Dying," *Long River Review*, 2023
"Ghazal for a Dispirited Place," *Small Orange Journal*, 2021
"Hunters & Collectors," *Stone Poetry Quarterly*, 2023
"If only I could choose my own country," *Stonecoast Review*, 2020
"Inaugural Poem, January 20, 2001," *Crab Orchard Review*, 2015
"Ineffable," *Little Patuxent Review*, 2022
"In Margherita's Kingdom," *Third Wednesday*, 2021
"Leaves Aim Toward Thunder," *Stone Poetry Quarterly*, 2023
"Lesson Plan," *Humans in the Wild (Swallow/Mythic Picnic)*, 2020
"The Lives I Save Are Never My Own," *Coal Hill Review*, 2019
"Lopsided," *petrichor: A Journal of Text & Image*, 2018
"Love Is a Graveyard for the Lonely," *Occulum*, 2020
"More's the Pity," *Anti-Heroin Chic*, 2018
"Mother Courage," *Kissing Dynamite*, 2019
"A Newspaper Headline Announces that the Big Bang Created a Mirror Universe Where Time Goes Backward" (formerly "In the Middle of Nowhere"), *Crab Fat Magazine*, 2019
"Parting Catechism (Prose Pantoum)" (formerly "Catechism or Parting Pantoum"), *Susurrus*, 2023
"Predicament," *Susurrus*, 2023
"Proof Through the Night" (formerly "Flag Guy"), *Iron Horse Literary Review, Newsflash*, 2018
"Psycho," *Rogue Agent*, 2022
"RSVP Is the Collective Noun for Snowy Egrets," *Split Rock Review*, 2019
"Reckoning," *Into the Void*, 2018
"Resurface," *Birdcoat Quarterly*, 2022
"Return," *North American Review*, 2023
"Sing Away, My Sister," *JMWW Anthology VII*, 2022

"A Slip Jig and Reel in Cut-Time," *Shenandoah*, 2017
"Spooky Little Things," *Stone Poetry Quarterly*, 2023
"Thanksgiving, Sunset," *Bear Review*, 2023
"The Sympathy of Clocks," *Five South*, 2022
"Things I Never Said," *Stone Poetry Quarterly*, 2023
"Tonight, the loon" (formerly "The loon wails"), *Half Mystic Journal*, 2019
"Unrhymed Sonnet Constructed with American Sentences," *Crack the Spine*, 2020
"The World Will Blow," *Unbroken*, 2020

Photography by Bill Ragsdale

Cate McGowan is an artist, critic, historian, and the author of three books. Her collection of memoir essays, *Writing is Revision*, will be published by *De Gruyter Brill* in 2024, and her novel, *These Lowly Objects*, appeared with *Gold Wake Press* in 2020. McGowan's short story collection, *True Places Never Are*, won the *Moon City Press* Short Fiction Award in 2014 and was a finalist for the Lascaux Prize. Cate's poetry, essays, and stories have appeared in numerous literary outlets, including *Norton's Flash Fiction International, Glimmer Train, The North American Review, Stonecoast Review, Chestnut Review, Shenandoah, Citron Review, Crab Orchard Review,* and *Tahoma Literary Review*. Professor McGowan (known as McG to her students) holds an M.F.A. and Ph.D. and is currently pursuing another advanced degree at Johns Hopkins University. She regards teaching as her lifeblood and lives in Florida with her husband and animal family, but remains deeply connected to her progressive Southern roots in Atlanta, Georgia.

MORE TITLES FROM
DRIFTWOOD PRESS

comics, fiction, poetry
chapbooks & collections

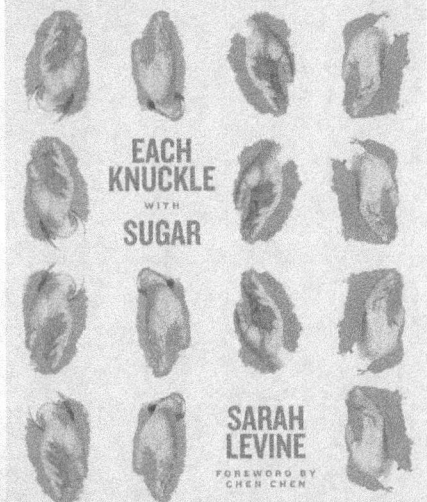
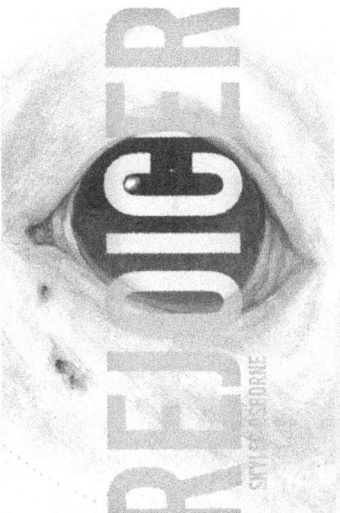

www.ingramcontent.com/pod-product-compliance
Lightning Source LLC
Chambersburg PA
CBHW081431070526
44586CB00020B/2552